Inside Australia's Simpson Desert

Meredith Hooper

CAMBRIDGE
UNIVERSITY PRESS

The author would like to thank Mark Shephard.

Contents

The Simpson Desert

The land is empty. The sky is wide and blue. In the distance there is a hill of sand, as high as a three-storey house. The sand is bright orange-red. The hill looks like a sand dune on a beach, except that there is no sea anywhere near because this is the middle of Australia.

Red sand spills across the stony earth at the bottom of the dune. Getting up the sand dune and down the other side is hard work. Ahead is another sand dune; beyond that another, and another. This is the Simpson Desert.

There are more than 1,100 dunes in the Simpson Desert. They rise up one behind another like waves in a sandy ocean. Some are 200 kilometres long.

5

Australia is the driest continent in the world, except for Antarctica.

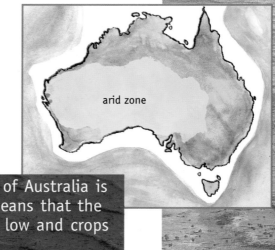

arid zone

Three-quarters of Australia is 'arid', which means that the rainfall is very low and crops cannot grow.

Great rivers once flowed across Australia. Then the land became drier and no water ran in the rivers. Winds blew sand away from the beds of the dry rivers. The sand collected into huge areas of sand dunes.

Tanami

Great Sandy

Gibson

Simpson

Great Victoria

Five sandy deserts cover nearly a quarter of Australia.

The Simpson Desert is the driest of all the dry places in Australia.

Simpson Desert

The Simpson Desert has the world's longest sand dunes.

There is almost no water and not much shade in the Simpson Desert. It is so hot that temperatures in summer can go up to 50 degrees Celsius (50 °C). Winter nights can be icy cold, with temperatures falling below freezing.

The Simpson Desert is huge, quiet, lonely and harsh.

Three large hunters

Dingo

It is early morning. A dingo runs across the red sand. She has been hunting all night. Dingoes can see well in the dark. Now the dingo is coming back to her pups, which are waiting in an old rabbit burrow.

The dingo feeds her pups. Then she goes to her daytime resting place under a shady bush.

Wedge-tailed eagle

High in the blue sky, a wedge-tailed eagle soars, searching the ground below for food. Its powerful wings are 2.5 metres (250 centimetres) from tip to tip.

The eagle lands on the crest of a sand dune and stares around with unwinking eyes. Its curved beak is strong. Its long legs are covered in brown feathers.

From the sand dune, the eagle can look down into its nest, which is in the top of an old tree. Inside the nest is one fluffy white chick.

9

Perentie

Late in the morning, a 2-metre-long lizard sways slowly across the sand. It is a perentie, the world's second-largest lizard. The shy perentie lives amongst rocks, coming out in the day to search for food. It eats anything it can get.

Large meat-eaters, like the dingo, wedge-tailed eagle and perentie, can live here in the Simpson Desert because there are enough animals amongst the sand dunes for them to eat.

People used to think that the desert was a dead place. Now they know that many different kinds of animals live in the desert, but it is not easy to see most of them.

One small hunter

Bush flies are easy to see. They crawl into your eyes and up your nose. They stick on your skin and clothes. Bush flies feed on protein, and humans have a good supply – protein is in our blood, saliva, sweat and tears.

Bush flies lay their eggs in piles of dung so that the maggots will have food as soon as they hatch.

Bush flies live all over Australia, even in the heat and dryness of the desert.

Plants

Silvery blue-green plants grow everywhere in the desert. The sides of sand dunes are covered with clumps of spinifex grass. Shrubs and trees grow in the flat spaces between the dunes.

Desert plants have ways of living with very little water.

The mulga tree's narrow leaves point upwards. Rain-water dribbles off the leaves, down the branches and trunk to the roots, so no water is wasted.

The witchetty bush is shaped like a funnel to catch every drop of rain.

Plants in the desert give animals
☀ homes
☀ shade and shelter
☀ food
Their roots help to stop the sand from blowing away.

Spinifex grows in spiky clumps on very poor soil or sand, surviving with very little rain. This grass covers a quarter of Australia.

In the Simpson Desert, spinifex sends long, stiff roots 3 metres down into the sand to search for water. Spinifex leaves are very spiky, which stops them from being eaten by most animals. The long sides of the leaf curl round tightly to form a hollow tube. This helps the spinifex to save moisture.

Termites

Some animals do eat the spiky spinifex. They are small and difficult to find, yet there are millions of them. They are called termites.

Termites live underground. Their homes are like huge cities, with entrances under clumps of spinifex. The little termites can control the air temperature and moisture in their underground tunnels and rooms.

At night, worker termites run around the spinifex, collecting dead leaves and dragging them underground. The leaves are cut into small pieces. Some are eaten, but many of them are stored in special rooms for times when the ground outside is too hot even for termites to work.

Soldier termites guard the nest. They have snapping jaws and big heads.

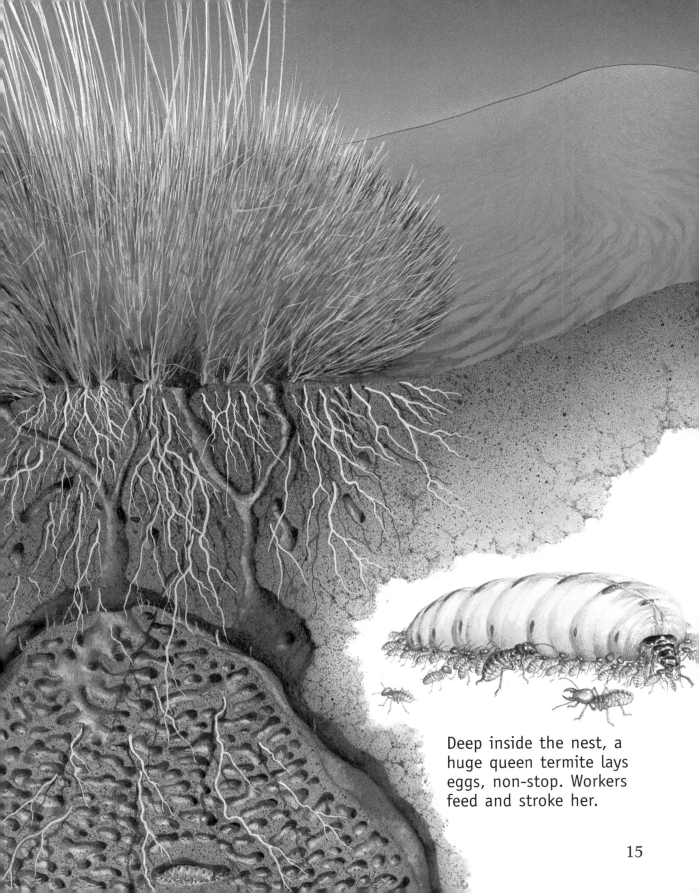

Deep inside the nest, a huge queen termite lays eggs, non-stop. Workers feed and stroke her.

15

Lizards

Australia has many more kinds of lizards than any other country. A large number of lizards live in the desert.

Lizards are meat-eaters. Some lizards eat termites and ants. Some eat insects, small animals or other lizards. Different lizards hunt at different times and in different places. Some lizards hunt at night, some in the day. Some rest in holes, others hide in the spinifex. Some burrow, some like being out in the open.

The bearded dragon sunbakes in the morning, warming its bright orange body before starting to search for insects. If the bearded dragon is disturbed, it puffs up, opens its mouth to look fierce, hisses and darkens its skin.

Geckoes have large bulging eyes which
help them to see in the dark. They clean
their eyes with their thick tongues.

← The thorny devil looks frightening
but it is timid and eats ants. Moisture
collects on its spines and trickles down
its skin to the corner of its mouth.

The big sand goanna digs for food with
its strong legs. It likes to eat other
lizards. But when it cannot catch lizards,
it crunches up scorpions, eggs and mice.

Surviving in the desert

The sun beats down. The sand is baking hot. Nothing seems to move. In summer, even at night, the temperature can stay very high.

Most animals in the harsh desert protect themselves from the hot sun. They rest in the heat, sheltering in holes or burrows, and eat when it is cooler. Some dig their own holes, but some steal the holes of other animals.

As darkness comes, the huge sky is filled with brilliant stars. The desert is very quiet. The hot sun has gone, and animals come out to hunt and feed.

In the morning, the animals' tracks can be seen in the sand.

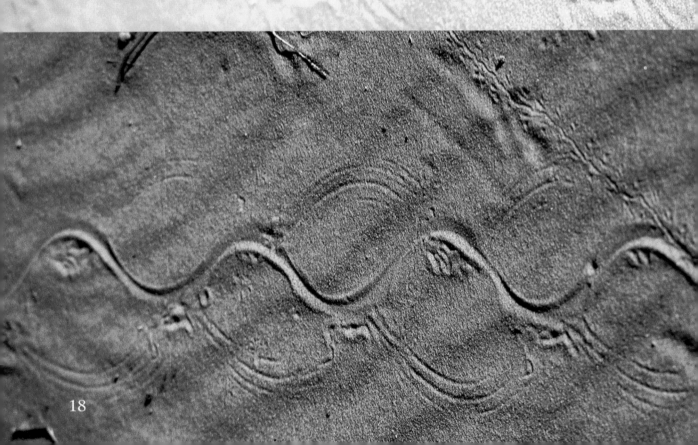

Desert scorpions hunt for spiders and ants. When night ends, the scorpions go down their spiral burrows and rest at the bottom, where they can keep cool and moist.

Wolf spiders wait at the top of their burrows. They reach out and grab at anything which comes near them.

Not many snakes live in the Simpson Desert. The king brown is one of the most venomous snakes in Central Australia. In cooler weather, it hunts in the day. In hot weather, it hunts at night.

Small, furry mammals scurry around at night, hunting for food. Some are very fierce, attacking with their sharp teeth.

The fat-tailed dunnart crunches up scorpions, spiders, even lizards. It can eat its own body weight of food in one night.

The spinifex hopping-mouse eats dry seeds. It hardly ever drinks. It uses its long legs and long tail to get away from its enemies, hopping and zigzagging across the sand. During the day, nine or ten spinifex hopping-mice sleep in the bottom of a burrow, huddled together.

Some mammals do hunt in the day.
  The short-beaked echidna snuffles
around, licking up termites and ants.

When the echidna wants
to protect itself, it rolls
up into a prickly ball.

  Life in the desert is difficult for the small
mammals. Many of them are eaten by other
animals. When no rain falls and the desert
gets drier and drier, they have to travel longer
and longer distances to find their food.

Rain

Sometimes, no rain falls in the desert for years. Then rain will fall. The rain can just sprinkle down, or pour.

When heavy rain comes, suddenly the red sand is covered in new life. Plants grow, birds flit and swoop, insects buzz, frogs croak.

Where does all the new life come from?

Seeds lie in the sand for years. As soon as the rain comes, the seeds sprout. The new plants have only a short time to grow, flower and make more seeds. In a few weeks, the sand dunes are covered in flowers.

Insects swarm. Some insects hatch from eggs that have been waiting for the rain.

Snails can stay inside their shells for years, waiting for rain. Now they come out and start eating.

Insect-eating birds swoop in to feed. Seed-eating birds dart across the desert looking for water. When the water has gone, they move away.

23

Deep down in the sand, there are
frogs. They have covered themselves in
a special outer cocoon of skin, like cling
film. Inside the cocoon they stay moist,
so they can wait underground for years.

Water trickles down through the sand
after heavy rain. When the water reaches
the frogs, they dig up to the surface.
Suddenly there are frogs leaping over
the sand, eating as much as they can,
and laying their eggs in pools of water.

Soon the muddy pools are seething
with tadpoles. Some of the tadpoles
grow into frogs.

As the water dries up, the frogs burrow down into the sand, cover themselves in their special cocoons of skin, and wait for the next rain to fall.

The thirsty desert soaks up the water like a sponge. In a few more weeks, the flowering plants dry out, leaving their seeds lying in the hot sun. Most of the birds have gone. Most of the insects die.

Animals that have disappeared

Many of the small mammals that used to live in the Simpson Desert are no longer there. Some have disappeared in just the last few years.

Bilbies have long ears and soft, silky fur. They come out of their burrows at night to dig for insects and seeds. But bilbies do not live in the Simpson Desert any more.

Stick-nest rats no longer live in the Simpson Desert. They used to build wonderful nests out of twigs and branches. The nests were a metre wide and nearly a metre high. In the middle of the nest there was a hole leading down to underground tunnels.

New arrivals

Now there are new kinds of wild animals living in the desert. They were brought to Australia during the last two hundred years. Some, like rabbits and cats, do terrible damage wherever they go in Australia.

Rabbits eat plants down to their roots. Rabbit holes break up the surface of the earth. Some native mammals probably starved because the rabbits ate their food.

Cats which have gone wild are called feral cats. They hunt at night, killing rabbits and other small animals.

For camels, the desert is → a wonderful home. Large herds of camels roam Central Australia. They eat leaves and bushes, which makes it harder for small mammals to find shelter.

Humans in the desert

Groups of Aboriginal people used to live in the
Simpson Desert all year round. They dug deep wells
down into soft sand to find water. They found their
food by hunting animals and collecting the seeds
of plants.

The Aborigines used to set fire to patches of spinifex.
These fires helped the plants and animals of the desert.
Many desert plants can sprout new leaves out of their
black, burnt stems. Others have seed pods which only
open after fire. Some desert animals feed on the new
shoots which grow after fire.

The Aborigines burnt patches of desert so that there
were always newly growing plants and food for the
animals they hunted.

Conservation

The desert is harsh, but it has a strange beauty. Today, people like to visit the desert. But it is best to go in the cooler winter. Even then, visitors must carry their own water, food, fuel and medical supplies. They must have maps and proper vehicles, and they should tell other people about their plans.

The desert has been changed by the animals which live in it. The desert has been changed by the way people use it. The desert looks strong. In fact, it is fragile. Sand dunes, and the plants growing on them, are easily damaged by tourists and their vehicles.

The desert needs to be protected and understood. Some areas of the Simpson Desert are now Parks, which helps to protect them. The Simpson Desert might soon become a World Heritage Site.

Index